Exponential Visual Guide

Fundamentals of Kingdom Multiplication

EXPONENTIAL

Exponential Visual Guide: Fundamentals of Kingdom Multiplication

Exponential's mission is The 16% Mission: to see a tipping point of 16% of churches in the U.S. becoming multiplying churches. We equip movement makers with actionable principles, ideas, and solutions for the accelerated multiplication of healthy, reproducing faith communities.

This book is manufactured in the United States.

ISBN-13: 978-1-62424-130-7

Editors: Jason Stewart and Bill Couchenour

Cover and Design by Sabir Robinson

Introduction

Welcome to this Journey!

I'm delighted to have you here! I truly believe we are on the verge of something significant—something inspired by the Spirit of God and propelled by courageous, Jesus-centered leaders like ourselves. There is a growing discontent with the status quo. The vision of the church as a movement is urging leaders like you and me to not only envision something greater but to actively engage in that journey.

I want to share an exciting initiative that's close to my heart—our 16% Mission. This mission aims to inspire 16% of churches in the United States to become reproducing churches that actively plant new congregations.

You may have heard that most church leaders recognize three levels of church health: declining, plateauing, and growing. However, we believe there are actually five levels, which include:

1. Level 1: Subtracting
2. Level 2: Plateauing
3. Level 3: Adding
4. Level 4: Reproducing (churches that plant new churches)
5. Level 5: Multiplying (churches that reproduce to four generations of new churches)

Our goal is to see 16% and beyond of churches reach Level 4 or 5 because we believe this percentage represents a crucial tipping point for a movement across the U.S. Research shows that brand new churches often see three to four times the conversions compared to those that have been around for over a decade. This isn't just about numbers; it's about providing every person with access to a life-changing relationship with Jesus.

Since we launched this mission, we've seen promising progress. In 2015, only 4% of churches were reproducing, but by 2019, that number had climbed to 7%. In our second study with Lifeway Research in 2025, we found the current rate of reproducing and multiplying over the last few years is holding at 7%. While we are glad we did not take a step back after the pandemic and other cultural challenges we have faced in the U.S. context, we know there is still more work to do—together—to reach the tipping point of 16%.

The key to our success lies in becoming Multipliers—healthy disciple-making leaders who champion reproduction. Multipliers come from all walks of life, whether in full-time ministry, co-vocational roles, or the marketplace. They aim to live a 100X life, creating ripple effects that extend far beyond their immediate reach.

But being a Multiplier isn't just about external growth; it's also about internal transformation. We want to see you thrive in every aspect of your life. Multipliers prioritize their families, cultivate strong marriages, and seek the expansion of God's Kingdom without sacrificing their well-being.

This journey is not always easy, but I firmly believe that with the right support and resources, you can embrace this calling. At Exponential, we're dedicated to equipping you to become a Multiplier and to help you nurture other Multipliers in your community.

We consider it a privilege to walk alongside you in this mission. Together, we can create a movement that changes lives and communities for generations to come.

I'm really excited about this resource. This Visual Guide contains many of the core frameworks and principles we have seen in the lives of countless Multipliers. I believe a movement is inside of you. And I believe this resource will be a catalyst for you and your friends on mission to start and sustain a movement for the Jesus mission.

Let's embark on this journey together!

Dave Ferguson

Co-founder and CEO, Exponential

Prayer for Our Journey Together

Father,

We come before You with grateful hearts, acknowledging the incredible journey ahead of us. Thank You for the call You have placed on our lives and for the vision You are stirring within us. As we stand on the brink of something significant, we ask for Your guidance and wisdom. Empower us with the courage to embrace this mission, inspired by Your Spirit.

Lord, we recognize the growing discontent with the status quo and the desire for change. Help us to engage actively in this movement, envisioning a future where 16% of churches are reproducing and planting new congregations. May our efforts not just increase numbers but provide countless individuals with access to a life-changing relationship with Jesus.

We pray for every leader joining this journey—may they feel Your presence as they navigate their excitement, nervousness, or apprehension. Grant them clarity, strength, and the passion to become Multipliers in their communities. Help us to cultivate healthy, disciple-making leaders who prioritize their families and seek Your Kingdom first.

As we move forward together, may we support and encourage one another, creating a ripple effect that extends far beyond our immediate reach. We trust in Your timing and Your plan, knowing that with Your help, we can create a lasting impact on lives and communities for generations to come.

Moving to Multiplication

Section I

God didn't call you to be a ministry manager. He called you to be a Multiplier!

A **Multiplier** is a healthy disciple-making leader who champions reproduction.

But...

WHAT IF
WE HAVE THE
WRONG TARGET

(or we have the wrong paradigm)

What's the math behind your paradigm?

Subtracting

Adding

Multiplying

The Five Levels of Multiplication

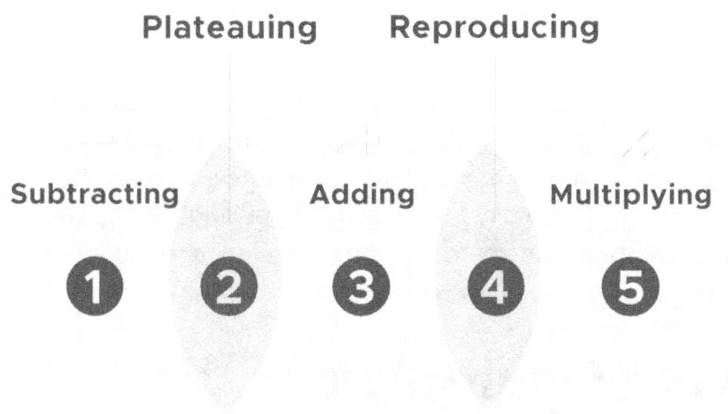

Level 1: Subtracting

Level 1 churches are characterized by subtraction, scarcity, and survival. They experience some combination of declining attendance, staffing, income, and conversions. Without a turnaround, Level 1 churches eventually close.

Level 2: Plateauing

Level 2 churches are plateaued and looking for the next catalyst to spark a season of growth. These churches experience some combination of flat attendance, staffing, income, and conversions. These churches may see temporary ups and downs, but their overall trend is flat.

Level 3: Adding

Level 3 churches are characterized by addition, growth, and expansion of impact. They have a strong growth culture with some combination of increasing attendance, staffing, income, and baptisms. Leadership development and conquering the next growth barriers are often key priorities in these churches.

Level 4: Reproducing

Level 4 churches are characterized by the value and priority they place on starting new churches—they have a strong programmatic emphasis on it. They see their fruit as more than the apples on their own tree, but by the other trees they plant in the orchard—or the new orchards they establish. These churches continually feel the tension pulling them toward investing in addition at their own church on the one hand, and the Kingdom expansion of new churches on the other.

Level 5: Multiplying

Level 5 churches are characterized by multiplying, releasing, and sending everyday missionaries and church planters. Multiplication is so deeply embedded in the DNA of these churches that they would need a strategy to stop multiplication. These churches plant churches that plant churches to the fourth generation, resulting in hundreds of churches in their multiplication family. They reach non-Christians at a much higher rate of conversion than other churches, and see disciple making to the fourth generation as a cultural norm.

The vast majority of churches (70–80%) find themselves in Levels 1 and 2. And most are striving to be Level 3.

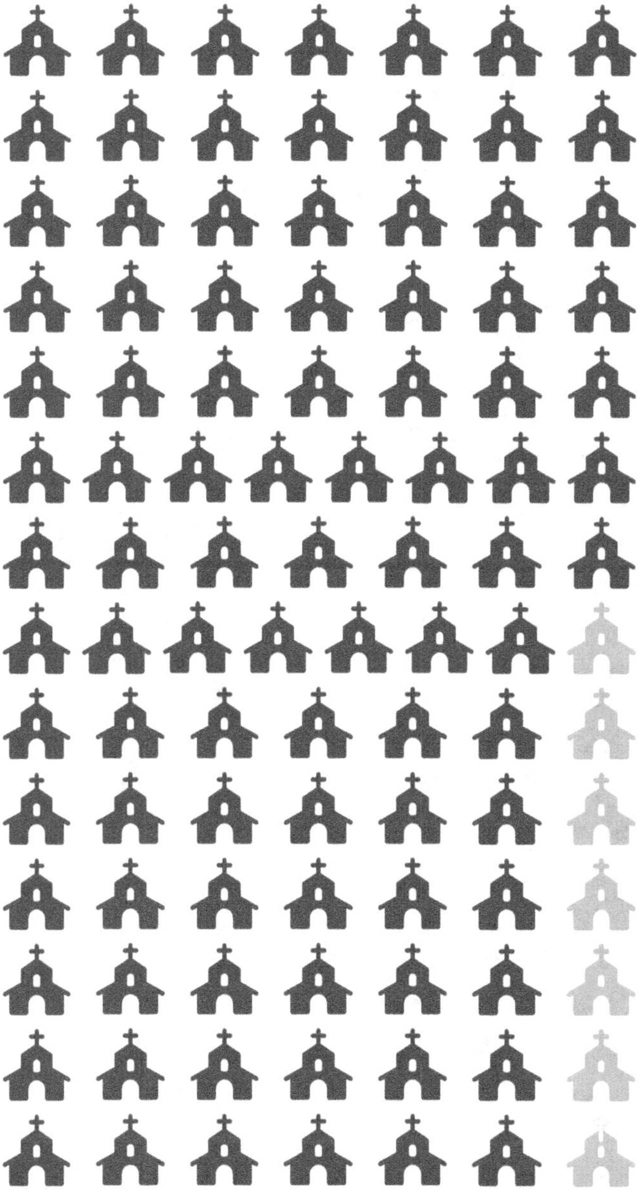

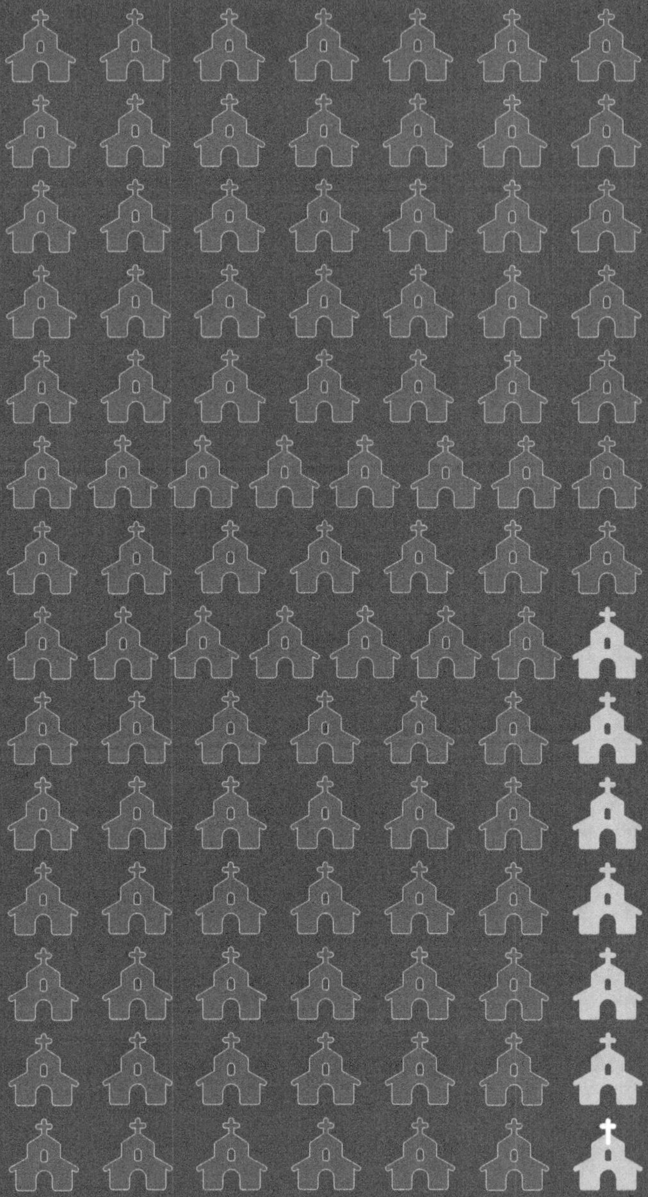

Only 7% of churches demonstrate Level 4 behaviors and Level 5 is less than .01%.

So, here's the reality...

Culture eats strategy for breakfast.

- PETER DRUCKER

Every church has a culture.

Which default culture are you experiencing?

Level 3 is good but Level 4 and Level 5 are greater!

But, Level 3 addition is the primary measure of success in the Church. Why?

There is a huge magnet at Level 3.

Say hello to the "Level 3 Magnet"

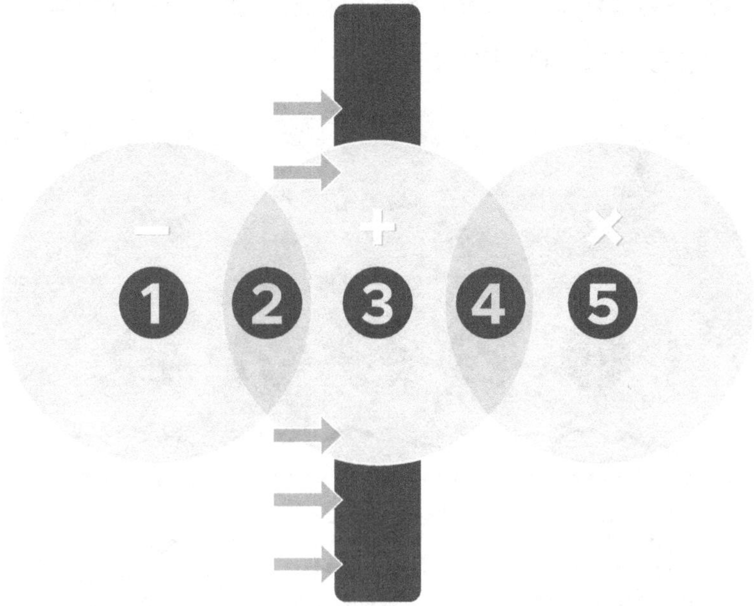

The magnet works both ways.

The values and decisions that move you to Level 3 can keep you from moving to Level 5.

What keeps you at Level 3?

WRONG TARGET

(paradigm)

LEADS TO

WRONG STRATEGY

How do we move from Level 3 to Level 4 Reproducing and Level 5 Multiplying?

The way through the "Level 3 Magnet" are the 3 Dimensions of Multiplication

What if the **results** of our ministry and calling were leading to movement?

3 Dimensions of Multiplication

Disciple-Making

The core mission of the Church is to see people transformed into the image of Jesus as disciples and become disciple-makers.

Mobilization

Deploying all members of the local church to be everyday missionaries where they live, work, learn, and play.

Capacity

Prioritizing the culture and resources in the local church to deploy and reproduce more disciples, missionaries, and churches.

GOING DEEPER
Read *2025 Becoming Five Multiplication Study Research Report* to learn more about moving into mobilization.
Visit exponential.org/books.

Disciple-Making

Section II

We are experiencing a wake-up call in the Church.

Although making disciples is the **clear mission** of the Church, when asked, most churches say that making disciples who make disciples is still their **biggest weakness**.

We sense **God is calling the Church to return to its primary purpose**, to make disciples who make disciples.

In order for us to do that we must make a one eighty turn with the following five shifts...

1. **From Reaching to Making**
2. **From Informing to Equipping**
3. **From Attending to Attaching**
4. **From Striving to Thriving**
5. **From Accumulating to Deploying**

Shift 1

From Reaching to Making

We need to shift from just reaching to **making disciples**.

1 From Reaching to Making

2 From Informing to Equipping

3 From Attending to Attaching

4 From Striving to Thriving

5 From Accumulating to Deploying

And he said to them, "Follow me, and I will make you fishers of men."

Go therefore and make disciples of all nations, baptizing them in the name of the Father and of the Son and of the Holy Spirit, teaching them to observe all that I have commanded you. And behold, I am with you always, to the end of the age.

MATTHEW 4:19; 28:19–20 ESV

1

From Reaching to Making

Making the Shift

Define A Disciple

If you don't ever define a disciple, then you don't know if you've ever made one.

Key Themes for Your Definition of A Disciple

Relational

Following Jesus is about being in a relationship with Him.

Transformational

Being with Jesus leads to personal change.

Commisional

Disciples are called to do the works of Jesus.

1

From Reaching to Making

Making the Shift

Develop Your Process

Spiritual development consists of stages, starting from the spiritually dead and progressing to spiritual infancy, childhood, young adulthood, and spiritual parenthood.

Stages of Spiritual Development

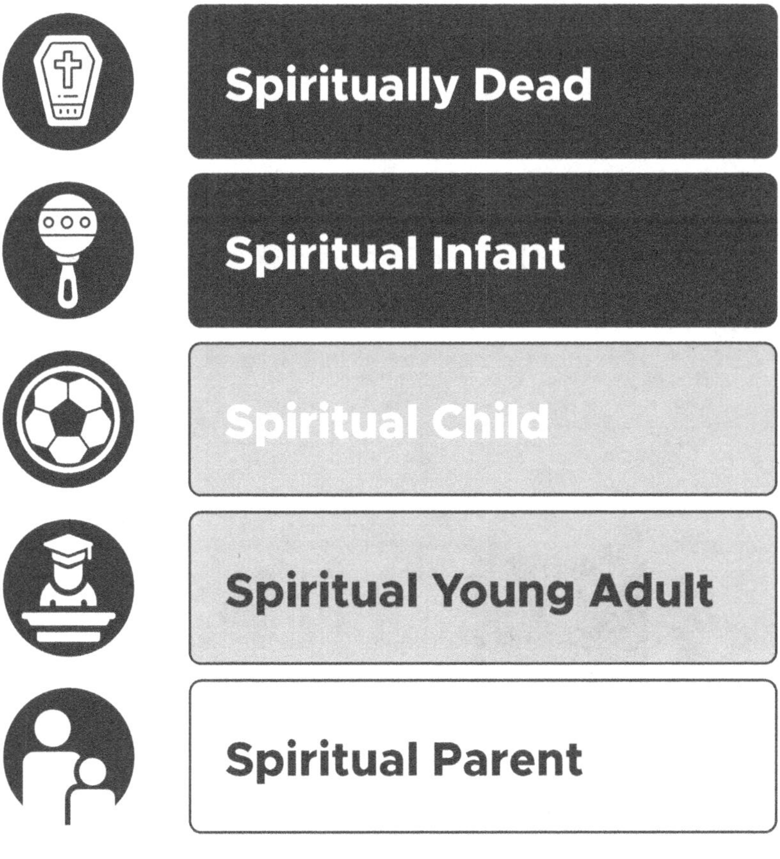

Shift 2

From Informing to Equipping

We need to shift from merely informing disciples to **equipping disciple-makers**.

1. From Reaching to Making
2. **From Informing to Equipping**
3. From Attending to Attaching
4. From Striving to Thriving
5. From Accumulating to Deploying

And he gave the apostles, the prophets, the evangelists, the shepherds and teachers, to equip the saints for the work of ministry, for building up the body of Christ, until we all attain to the unity of the faith and of the knowledge of the Son of God, to mature manhood, to the measure of the stature of the fullness of Christ, so that we may no longer be children, tossed to and fro by the waves and carried about by every wind of doctrine, by human cunning, by craftiness in deceitful schemes.

EPHESIANS 4:11-14

2

From Informing to Equipping

Making the Shift

Equipping God's People

If we are going to make a shift from informing to equipping, we are going to have to embrace the calling to see every disciple of Jesus set free and empowered to be a gift and to equip others as gifts.

Leaders must empower people for active engagement and transformation in their faith.

- Model a life of being a disciple of Jesus
- Provide experiential learning opportunities
- Build deep relationships with individuals
- Address the heart and character of individuals
- Create a culture of reflection, grace, and growth
- Empower individuals to do the works of Jesus

2

From Informing to Equipping

Making the Shift

The D.E.E.P.E.R. Equipping Process

We need true holistic equipping. Informing is the least effective way. We want to equip in such a way that we can send people out to start new spiritual families.

The Equipping Process

Demonstrate (See It)
Experience (Taste It)
Explain (Hear It)
Practice (Do It)
Expose (Reveal It)
Reflect (Process It)

Repeat this process until they can Reproduce it in others.

Shift 3

From Attending to Attaching

We need to shift from calling people to attend programs and events, to **leading** people to **truly attach to God and others**.

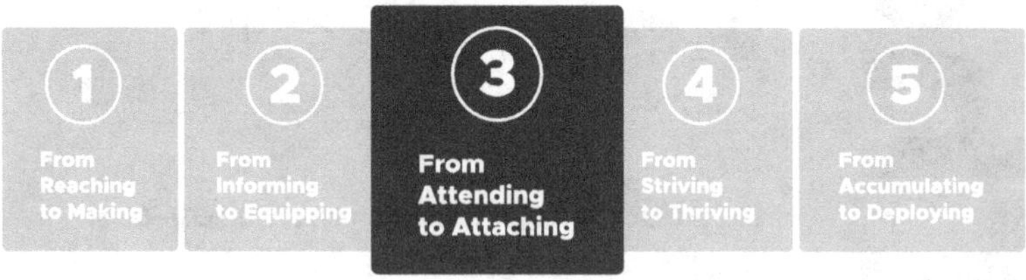

Abide in me, and I in you. As the branch cannot bear fruit by itself, unless it abides in the vine, neither can you, unless you abide in me. I am the vine; you are the branches. Whoever abides in me and I in him, he it is that bears much fruit, for apart from me you can do nothing.

JOHN 15:4-5 ESV

“

3

From Attending to Attaching

Making the Shift

Creating Disciple-Making Spaces

Disciple-making should lead to attachment love with God, self, and others. We must create disciple-making spaces that foster attachment through intimate relationships, personal reflection, and engagement with God.

Creating Disciple-Making Spaces

Space	Description	Primary Outcome	In the Life of Jesus
Divine Space	One-on-one encounter with God, communion with the Father	Intimate attachment to God's love, transformation into the image of Jesus	Jesus often withdrawing to solitary places to be alone with the Father
Transparent Space	2–4 people, complete openness and vulnerability	Shared truth, deep friendship, and acceptance	Jesus having a few close friends (Peter, James, and John) whom He became transparent with
Personal Space	4–12 people, sharing personal information and experiences	Practicing the "one anothers", doing life together in community	Jesus spending time with His twelve disciples and close followers
Social Space	20–70 people, building affinity with others	Neighborly relations, starting closer friendships	Jesus attending parties and gatherings, inviting people into community
Public Space	100s–1,000s engaging with something outside us rather than building relational depth	Shared experience, gathering in crowds who have similar interests and pursuits, fans seeking entertainment	Jesus speaking to the crowds, feeding them, but calling some to follow Him

3

From Attending to Attaching

Making the Shift

Growing in Love Through Spiritual Practices

Jesus invites us to walk in His way, and His way is the way of love, laying down His life out of love for us. The spiritual practices are meant to lead us into the way and to attachment love with God and others.

Growing in Love Through Spiritual Practices

Space	Spiritual Practices	Desired Outcome
Divine Space	Reading the Bible, prayer, silence, and solitude	Attach to God, renew minds, feed souls, attune ears to God's voice
Transparent Space	Daily examen, giving thanks, confession, and surrender	Be aware of God's presence, express feelings and needs, receive God's grace
Personal Space	Practicing the "one anothers"	Practicing the "one anothers", doing life together in community
Social Space	Hospitality, loving the stranger, making others feel at home	Provide a loving welcome, create space for others to be themselves, rest from performance and striving
Public Space	Sunday gathering, liturgy, singing, and teaching	Lead people to know and experience God

Shift 4

From Striving to Thriving

We need to shift from unhealthy striving to thriving as **spirit-empowered disciples and emotionally healthy leaders.**

1 From Reaching to Making

2 From Informing to Equipping

3 From Attending to Attaching

4 From Striving to Thriving

5 From Accumulating to Deploying

But I say, walk by the Spirit, and you will not gratify the desires of the flesh. But the fruit of the Spirit is love, joy, peace, patience, kindness, goodness, faithfulness, gentleness, self-control; against such things there is no law. And those who belong to Christ Jesus have crucified the flesh with its passions and desires. If we live by the Spirit, let us also keep in step with the Spirit.

GALATIANS 5:16; 22-25 ESV

“

4

From Striving to Thriving

Making the Shift

Spirit-Empowered Ministry

Without the Spirit, our efforts will wear us out. We need to walk in the power of the Spirit.

We are commanded by Jesus to make disciples and teach them to obey everything He commanded. That includes being filled, led, and empowered by the Spirit to do the same works Jesus did.

Empowered by Love

Jesus began His ministry in a place of dependency so that He could receive the anointing of the Spirit. He also did not engage in ministry to gain the Father's approval. He started with a full tank of affection. He had all the power and all the love to go forward in ministry.

Empowered to Overcome

Jesus overcame temptation by resting in the Father's love, knowing the Scriptures, and being filled by the Spirit.

Empowered to Speak

The Gospel writer Luke wants us to see that Jesus was able to do so because He was filled and anointed with the Holy Spirit. This same phenomenon occurs when Jesus-followers are anointed and filled with the Holy Spirit after He ascends.

Empowered for the Miraculous

Jesus had promised that those who believed in Him would also do what He did by the power of the same Spirit who enabled Him.

4

From Striving to Thriving

Making the Shift

Your Journey

Health is crucial for leaders. Too many leaders are not relationally, physically, mentally, and spiritually healthy. As a result, they do not have a life worth emulating. We need to take our own personal journey seriously and learn to thrive in our relationship with God and prioritize self-care.

Your Journey

How healthy is your leadership? How emotionally and relationally healthy are you? Ask those around you what it's like to be on the other side of you.

The kind of disciples we make is shaped by the kind of leaders we are and the cultures we create. Jesus said, "Everyone who is fully trained will be like their teacher."

You have very real needs and desires. If you are not attending to them or are meeting them in appropriate ways, they will war within you, destroying your internal world. Your unattended needs and desires find destructive ways to seek satisfaction that will also destroy your outside world.

Shift 5

From Accumulating to Deploying

We need to shift from merely accumulating people into our buildings and programs to **deploying disciple-making leaders** to the ends of the Earth.

1	2	3	4	5
From Reaching to Making	From Informing to Equipping	From Attending to Attaching	From Striving to Thriving	**From Accumulating to Deploying**

and what you have heard from me in the presence of many witnesses entrust to faithful men, who will be able to teach others also.

2 TIMOTHY 2:2 ESV

”

For whoever would save his life will lose it, but whoever loses his life for my sake will find it.

MATTHEW 16:25 ESV

”

5

From
Accumulating
to Deploying

Making the Shift

Changing the Scorecard

You measure and celebrate what you value. And the people you lead and the disciples they make will be formed by the scorecard you keep.

What was Jesus' scorecard? What did He measure? How did the early church embrace that same scorecard?

Let's reframe our measurements to look less like the kingdom of this world to resemble the Kingdom of God.

- Love of God, self, and others
- Disciple-making relationships (believers and non-believers)
- Generosity of spirit and possessions
- Care for the poor, the lonely, the lost, equipping and mobilizing every believer for ministry
- Releasing and sending (as opposed to just numbers gathering)

5

From Accumulating to Deploying

Making the Shift

Surrender—This Starts with You

The change begins in you. The best step forward is repentance and faith leading to obedience to Jesus. We all need to start with surrender.

Surrender Personally

Turn back to God in any way you have grown distant or detached.

Surrender to Make Disciples

Embrace the personal call to make disciples in your context.

Surrender the Ministry

Commit to take steps to create a disciple-making culture that equips, releases, and sends.

Surrender to be Sent

Commit to start a new ministry or church that will exist for the primary purpose of making disciples who make disciples.

Don't give up.

Jesus promised He would build his church, and the gates of hell (and our past mistakes) will not prevail against His work.

You can be a part of the way Jesus accomplishes His will and His work in this generation.

GOING DEEPER

Read *One Eighty: A Return to Disciple-Making* to learn more about disciple-making.

Visit exponential.org/books.

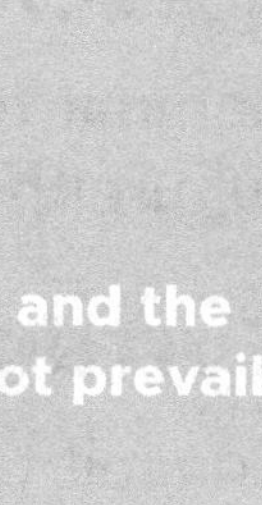

Mobilization

Section III

mo•bi•lize verb

1. prepare and organize for active service
2. make something movable or capable of movement.

Mobilization is the bridge between disciple-making and multiplication movements!

Every believer and every church was "made for more"; made to be "mobilized", made for "active service" in moving the Kingdom of God forward in the world; made to help multiply disciple-making and churches.

With only 7% of churches reproducing, we have a serious mobilization problem.

Our mobilization problem starts in the hearts and minds of church leaders!

- Our accumulation based operating systems must change.
- Our personal and church scorecards of success must change.
- Our programmatic approach to adding disciples must be replaced with Jesus' style of relational disciple-making.

Leaders must shift from a bias of "we can do it, you can help" to one of "you can do it, how can we help?"

Examining Ephesians

Creating a Culture of Mobilization

Paul's letter to the church in Ephesus **reveals truths** we need to embrace **and shifts** we need to make.

Examining Ephesians 1

We need to embrace the truth and mystery that the fullness of Jesus can fill every corner of society through the Church.

TRUTH 1

And God placed all things under His feet and appointed Him to be head over everything for the church, which is His body, the fullness of Him who fills everything in every way.

EPHESIANS 1:22-23

The Church is made for MORE!

Only Jesus can fill everything in every way.

He chose the Church and his followers to be his ambassadors to carry His fullness into every crack and cranny of society!

A core commitment of every local church is to continually illuminate this mystery: Jesus is More. Therefore, the Church is Made for More. The Church is chosen by Jesus to express His fullness into every corner of culture and into every sphere of society.

TRUTH 1

MAKING IT PERSONAL

Jesus is MORE.

FROM...

The "We Can Do It. You Can Help." operating system for mobilization is characterized by...

worship services, teaching, and events. Join us to worship, listen to great teachers, and participate in programs. The bias of our church is "Come and do!"

TO...

The "You Can Do It. We Can Help." operating system is characterized by...

being a disciple of Jesus. You are called to live a lifestyle of worship and mission in every area of life—where you live, work, learn, and play. By embracing Jesus' Lordship and applying the Gospel daily, you'll be equipped to share it with others and reveal His fullness in all areas of culture and society. The direction of our church is "Go and be!"

Shift 1

We must shift our culture from more effort to more Jesus.

More effort means...

- Merely human effort producing human results.
- Over-reliance on charisma, stamina, ingenuity, or titles.
- Token prayer at the start or end of meetings.
- The Gospel is shared occasionally, with an altar call on weekends.
- Mobilization focuses on finding enough volunteers to keep things running.

More Jesus means...

- Start from a place of rest in the Gospel and identity in Christ.
- Depend radically on the Spirit through deep listening and responding.
- Pray without ceasing, moving forward only as fast as we can on our knees.
- Share the Gospel daily, first with ourselves, then with others.
- Mobilize by helping people discover their calling and equipping them as everyday missionaries in their communities.

Examining Ephesians 2

We need to embrace the truth that every follower of Jesus is a masterpiece work of God with a general calling and a unique calling.

TRUTH 2

For we are God's handiwork, created in Christ Jesus to do good works, which God prepared in advance for us to do.

EPHESIANS 2:10

The Church is made to BE more!

Every disciple is a unique, handcrafted-by-God vessel for expressing the fullness of Jesus into every corner of culture and into every sphere of society.

A core commitment of the local church is to help disciples investigate their masterpiece: their personal calling to a one-of-a-kind Masterpiece Mission for More.

TRUTH 2

MAKING IT PERSONAL

The Church is made to BE more.

FROM...

The "We Can Do It. You Can Help." operating system for mobilization is characterized by...

guiding attenders in discovering their unique design, helping them find volunteer opportunities that align with their God-given gifts, passions, and story. Ministry happens through various church programs, primarily at our facility or partner organization locations. The direction of our church is "Come, join us!"

TO...

The "You Can Do It. We Can Help." operating system is characterized by...

The "You Can Do It. We Can Help." operating system for mobilization is characterized by helping every person discover their unique masterpiece mission as a disciple of Jesus, designed to reveal His fullness. Ministry isn't limited to the church—it's about activating God's people to serve in every area of culture and society. The direction of our church is "Go and be!"

Shift 2

We must shift our culture from seeing people as volunteers to seeing them as unique masterpieces with a mission.

More volunteer means...

- Ministry equals volunteerism a few hours a month.
- Engaging ministry involves inviting people to join a local church or partner organization's program.
- Viewing people as a way to support church programs and fulfill a vision defined by a select few.

More masterpiece means...

- Ministry equals all of life and happens mostly where we live, work, learn, and play.
- Engaging ministry requires with everyone being a disciple who makes disciples and fulfills their personal calling.
- Staff should focus on equipping people to discover their calling and deploying them where they can best fulfill it.

Examining Ephesians 3

We need to embrace the truth that our primary motivation for mobilization is love!

TRUTH 3

I pray that out of his glorious riches he may strengthen you with power through his Spirit in your inner being, so that Christ may dwell in your hearts through faith. And I pray that you, being rooted and established in love, may have power, together with all the Lord's holy people, to grasp how wide and long and high and deep is the love of Christ, and to know this love that surpasses knowledge - that you may be filled to the measure of all the fullness of God. Now to Him who is able to do immeasurably more than all we ask or imagine, according to his power that is at work within us, to him be glory in the church and in Christ Jesus throughout all generations, for ever and ever! Amen.

EPHESIANS 3:16–21

The Church is made to LOVE more!

His love is the only sufficient motivation for our mission to More.

Primary (General) Calling

To express the fullness of Jesus to others, we must have the fullness of Jesus in us. We grow in this fullness by being disciples ourselves (BE), who make disciples of others (DO), wherever we go (GO). This is the primary (general) calling all disciples have in common.

Secondary (Unique) Calling

Our personal (unique) calling, on the other hand, distinguishes us from all other disciples. The personal calling ONLY finds its significance within the context of our primary calling to be disciples, who make disciples, wherever we go.

TRUTH 3

MAKING IT PERSONAL

The Church is made to LOVE more.

FROM...

The "We Can Do It. You Can Help." operating system for mobilization is characterized by...

inspiring action that emphasizes urgency and the importance of making a difference, focusing on DO and GO.

TO...

The "You Can Do It. We Can Help." operating system is characterized by...

inspiring people to understand their identity in Christ and the difference He has already made. Our focus on BE, DO, and GO equips disciples to embrace the Great Commission, combining their primary calling to share the Gospel with their personal calling to reflect Jesus in all areas of culture and society.

Shift 3

We must shift our culture from more guilt to more love.

More guilt means...

- The staff continually needs to "pump" people up to fill the necessary slots.
- People often feel ministry is something they "should" do, and we run a big recruitment campaign once a year.
- Volunteer burnout is common and usually addressed reactively by suggesting a break, instead of proactively prioritizing spiritual formation. A new volunteer is then found to fill the role.

More love means...

- As leaders, our priority is to abide in Jesus' presence and rest in His love. For those we lead, our goal is to equip them to know how to do the same.
- Ministry becomes a natural overflow of their life with Jesus, and they see it as an honor to join His mission where they live, work, learn, and play. People take new steps in ministry without needing external pressure.
- We follow daily, weekly, and annual rhythms of work and rest, staying aligned with God's design, as reflected in Jesus' life.

Examining Ephesians 4

We need to embrace the truth that our organizational structures should equip and deploy everyday missionaries.

TRUTH 4

So Christ himself gave the apostles, the prophets, the evangelists, the pastors and teachers, to equip His people for works of service, so that the body of Christ may be built up until we all reach unity in the faith and in the knowledge of the Son of God and become mature, attaining to the whole measure of the fullness of Christ. Then we will no longer be infants, tossed back and forth by the waves, and blown here and there by every wind of teaching and by the cunning and craftiness of people in their deceitful scheming. Instead, speaking the truth in love, we will grow to become in every respect the mature body of Him who is the head, that is, Christ. From Him the whole body, joined and held together by every supporting ligament, grows and builds itself up in love, as each part does its work.

EPHESIANS 4:11-16

The Church is made to DO more!

Jesus has provided a mosaic of unique gifts.

Regardless of our theology on specific gifts, we are wise to at least consider the pragmatic wisdom in the strengths represented within the functions of gifts mentioned in describing the church and its people. We must see the unique roles within the gifts given by Jesus as important considerations when designing the organizing systems of the church lest we miss key functions he intended.

TRUTH 4

MAKING IT PERSONAL

The Church is made to DO more.

FROM...

The "We Can Do It. You Can Help." operating system for mobilization is characterized by...
organizing around one or two, instead of all five functions, described in Ephesians 4:11-12. Typically, these one or two rise to the top because they are the couple our pastor or leadership feels most comfortable with. These functions include Apostolic (pioneering/entrepreneurial), Prophetic (justice/mission), Evangelistic (outreach/inclusion), Shepherding (care/health), and Teaching (doctrine/systems). Churches also tend to measure success around attendance, buildings, and cash (the "ABCs"), and primarily equip people only in the areas and programs leaders prioritize.

TO...

The "You Can Do It. We Can Help." operating system is characterized by...
focusing on all five functions of "A.P.E.S.T." from Ephesians 4:11-12, aiming to reflect the fullness of Jesus. The primary dashboard is built around each of the functions found in Ephesians 4:11-12 while equipping disciples to identify and embrace their unique influencing style and valuing the diversity of functions in the Church.

Shift 4

We must shift our culture from professional clergy doing the work of ministry to equipping and deploying everyday missionaries on mission.

More hierarchy means...

- Pastors and staff lead most ministries, with members supporting their work.
- New "ministries" must be approved before taking action.
- Staff are evaluated on their ministry's effectiveness.

More missionaries means...

- Members view their daily lives—where they live, work, learn, and play—as their main ministry. They are also eager to support the church's shared ministry through centralized programs.
- Members are constantly launching new ministry initiatives without expecting "the church" to do it, fund it, or centralize it.
- The staff is evaluated on how well they equip others in their ministry and mission.

Examining Ephesians 5

We need to embrace the truth that our primary mission fields are outside the walls of the church.

TRUTH 5

For you were once darkness, but now you are light in the Lord. Live as children of light... This is why it is said: "Wake up, sleeper, rise from the dead, and Christ will shine on you." Be very careful, then, how you live - not as unwise but as wise, making the most of every opportunity, because the days are evil. Therefore, do not be foolish, but understand what the Lord's will is.

EPHESIANS 5:8–17

The Church is made to GO more!

Mission begins by expressing the fullness of Jesus where we live, work, study, and play.

The people of God have already been sent and placed strategically by Jesus.

Our "GO" is to embrace our mission field and "make the most of every opportunity" to express the fullness of Jesus to others.

Every disciple is a missionary with a unique mission field, their mosaic of mission. All those overlapping mosaics of mission are Jesus' plan to express His fullness into every corner of culture and into every sphere of society. Each mosaic significantly extends the "footprint of fullness."

TRUTH 5

MAKING IT PERSONAL

The Church is made to GO more.

FROM . . .

The "We Can Do It. You Can Help." operating system for mobilization is characterized by...

actively encouraging everyone to get involved in church programs, emphasizing opportunities like short-term mission trips and service projects in the inner city. We celebrate and publicly share the stories of our volunteers to inspire others, and we strive to make it simple for people to take their first steps into ministry and mission work.

TO . . .

The "You Can Do It. We Can Help." operating system is characterized by ...

a commitment to engaging all areas of culture and society with a missionary mindset. This includes calling individuals to embrace their purpose where they live, work, learn, and play, celebrating and sharing stories of those who live out their calling, and equipping them to navigate the challenges of a missionary lifestyle with community support and soul care.

Shift 5

We must shift our culture from a program based "come and see" to a disciple-making "go and be" approach.

More programs means...

- We rely on centralized, church-led programs to reach the world.
- Pastors and professionals determine the best ways to impact the community.
- Excellence and impact come through well-executed programs.
- Paid clergy control the ministry.

More mission fields means...

- We equip missionaries to form communities on mission, making disciples in new contexts.
- The Holy Spirit leads people to serve their communities, with church leaders offering support.
- Programs are streamlined, but our greatest hope is in releasing God's people to live on mission.
- Discipleship pathways equip and send people to start ministry beyond church control.

Examining Ephesians 6

We need to embrace the truth that we will face spiritual opposition when seeking to mobilize God's people, God's way.

TRUTH 6

Finally, be strong in the Lord and in His mighty power. Put on the full armor of God, so that you can take your stand against the devil's schemes. For our struggle is not against flesh and blood, but against the rulers, against the authorities, against the powers of this dark world and against the spiritual forces of evil in the heavenly realms.

EPHESIANS 6:10–12

The Church is made to WIN more!

The enemy will do everything possible to thwart God's plans for mobilizing His people, His way!

To win, we must consecrate ourselves for Jesus and His mission.

Individually

The enemy will attempt to hinder the fullness in us, restricting the expression of this fullness carried to others.

Corporately

When Paul speaks of "principalities and powers," this is another way of saying systems of oppression influenced by the demonic.

Often these systems are operating **INSIDE** the church.

TRUTH 6

MAKING IT PERSONAL

The Church is made to WIN more.

The "We Can Do It. You Can Help." operating system is characterized by...

a deep understanding of spiritual needs, we recognize the church as more than a structure, but a means to serve people. We provide professionals to aid spiritual growth and help individuals resist temptations. Through boosting prayer life and encouraging involvement, we equip each person in their spiritual battles.

The "You Can Do It. We Can Help." operating system for mobilization is characterized by...

regularly declaring and training people to see the church as a body, not a building, and as an everyday mission, not just events. It rejects the clergy/laity divide as outdated and calls leaders to measure success by equipping all believers for ministry. With strategic prayer and the prophetic use of God's Word, we advance together, knowing the gates of Hell will not prevail.

Shift 6

We must shift our culture from more strategy to more prayer, fasting, and surrender.

More strategy means...

- We quickly plug people into a discipleship plan; those who need extra grace can seek out counseling.
- We plan and pray for God to bless our strategy.
- We work hard to push the plan forward despite challenges.

More surrender means...

- We first root people in their identity in Christ, healing, and freedom as essential to discipleship.
- We pray and listen for the Spirit's direction, letting planning flow from discernment.
- We recognize the spiritual battle and rely on God's armor, not just human effort, to prevail.

GOING DEEPER

Read *Made for More: Six Essential Shifts for Creating a Culture of Mobilization* to learn more about moving into mobilization.
Visit exponential.org/books.

Deep Breath

Don't be discouraged!

These shifts don't happen overnight.

Keep showing up, keep making the shifts—momentum builds, and the flywheel starts to turn.

fly·wheel noun

A heavy revolving wheel in a machine which is used to increase the machine's momentum and thereby provide greater stability or a reserve of available power.

The Principle of the Flywheel

The Flywheel is difficult to turn at first, requiring extra focus and energy. It must turn against the position of rest, the status quo, inertia. The Flywheel turns slowly at first but begins to acquire increased momentum with each revolution until it is not only easily turning but actually increasing the momentum.

“

No matter how dramatic the end result, good-to-great transformations never happen in one fell swoop. In building a great company or social sector enterprise, there is no single defining action, no grand program, no one killer innovation, no solitary lucky break, no miracle moment. Rather, the process resembles relentlessly pushing a giant, heavy flywheel, turn upon turn, building momentum until a point of breakthrough, and beyond.

–JIM COLLINS

The Mobilization Flywheel

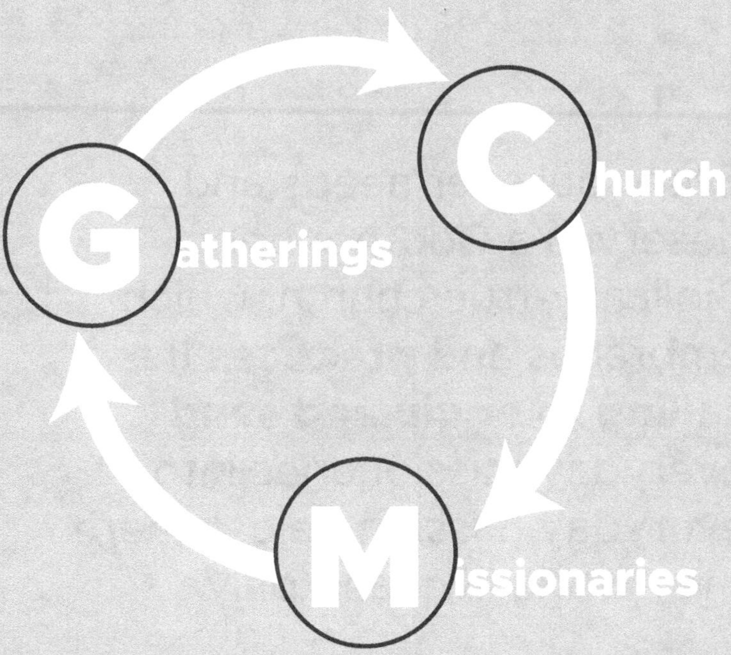

Church

Every believer needs and deserves a God-honoring, Biblically-true church, which embraces and **practices its calling** to **equip and send** everyday missionaries into everyday mission fields where they work, live, and play.

We are born again not only into Christ but into His family, the Church.

The church is a spiritual home...

- for receiving and giving love,
- for comforting and challenging one another,
- for discovering and discerning God's truth together,
- for being impacted by the gifts of one another,
- for submitting to God's anointed leaders and learning their ways of life,
- for operating on mission together,
- or being sent by the family to extend the family.

The church is both the starting point and the destination for the mobilization of believers.

The Church is our **home base** and **launch pad** for mobilization!

The Mobilization Flywheel begins with the Church because **the Church shapes how believers see themselves and what they**:

- expect of themselves and one another
- are trained to do
- are commissioned into
- celebrate and consequently, repeat

The core purpose of the Church is disciple-making.

In a mobilizing church, Jesus' method of relational disciple-making is the normative approach to addition.

The church is a family bound together by their primary or common calling to BE disciples, who make disciples (DO), in the everyday mission fields where they work, live, study, and play (GO).

M

Missionaries

Until the Church majors in equipping and sending ordinary Believers as **everyday missionaries**, we're unlikely to see sustainable multiplication movements.

Everyday Missionaries

For we are God's handiwork, created in Christ Jesus to do good works, which God prepared in advance for us to do.

EPHESIANS 2:10

100% of believers have the calling and the ability to be everyday missionaries with everyday mission fields where they work, live, and play!

What does an everyday missionary do?

An everyday missionary:

- Declares a circle of influence (mission field /unique context)
- Sees themselves as sent; a messenger and living ambassador of God to carry the fullness of Jesus to their unique circle of influence
- Carries a burden and urgency for the lost within their unique circle of influence
- Sees and understands the people and needs around them, and takes specific actions to meet needs within their unique circle of influence
- Prays and fasts for the people and needs around them, and for specific disciple-making opportunities
- Looks for opportunities to build relationships within their unique circle of influence
- Looks for opportunities to engage in relational disciple-making

The Challenge

Our programmatically-driven approach to adding disciples produces an over reliance on volunteerism to fuel the internal operations of the church.

This is one of the top tensions a church will face in seeking to mobilize God's people, God's way.

We must shift our paradigm from recruiting volunteers to accomplish "our thing" to mobilizing everyday missionaries in their common and unique callings to accomplish "God's thing."

Gatherings

What happens when an everyday missionary impacts their mission field?

gath·er·ings noun

A group of two or more people convened around faith, meeting together to discover and obey God's truths and purposes for their lives and in their world.

Where two or three gather in my name, there am I with them.

MATTHEW 18:20

A gathering includes at least one function of a healthy church and puts priority on obedience-based disciple-making.

- Bible study
- Prayer
- Fellowship
- Accountability
- Service
- Worship
- Skill development
- Training
- etc.

Most everyday missionaries can form and lead gatherings.

100% of everyday missionaries can play a role in gatherings.

Capacity

Section IV

Culture eats strategy for lunch

...breakfast and dinner, too

?

Is your culture aligned for multiplication?

They devoted themselves to the apostles' teaching and to fellowship, to the breaking of bread and to prayer. Everyone was filled with awe at the many wonders and signs performed by the apostles. All the believers were together and had everything in common. They sold property and possessions to give to anyone who had need. Every day they continued to meet together in the temple courts. They broke bread in their homes and ate together with glad and sincere hearts, praising God and enjoying the favor of all the people. And the Lord added to their number daily those who were being saved.

ACTS 2:42–47

What were the core values and convictions that shaped their stories and their practices?

A powerfully aligned culture increases the devotion of insiders and fuels the addition of outsiders to join the cause.

"they devoted themselves..."

"everyone was filled with awe..."

"believers were together and had everything in common..."

"praising God and enjoying the favor of all people..."

"the Lord added to their number daily..."

We need a powerfully aligned culture like we see in the Book of Acts.

Every culture regardless of its context shares three common elements:

1. a unique and distinctive set of core **values**.
2. a unique language and **narrative** that continually celebrates and communicates those values.
3. clear expectations, practices and **behaviors** that bring those values to life in tangible ways for people.

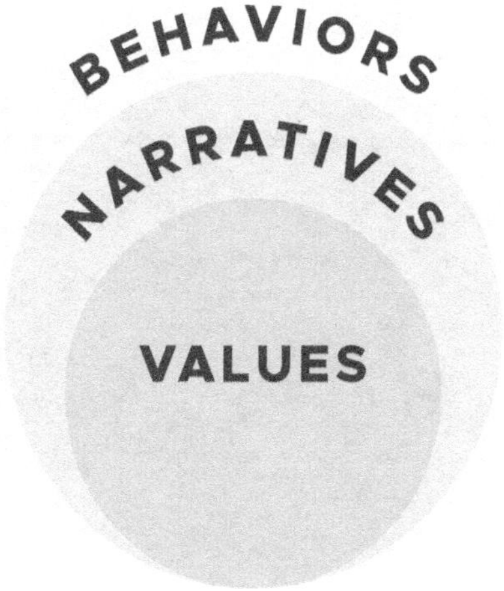

Culture Element 1

Values and Core Convictions

Values

- What's important to us
- Spoken and unspoken
- More caught than taught

What is the most important thing we need to be doing or what we are about right now?

What is important enough to us that it transcends all we do and shoes how we do what we do?

Values are...

...like a magnetic force field surrounding the people and operations of the church, proactively shaping the things to come and correcting the things that go off track.

...shown as the center circle because they bring life, meaning and context to the other elements of narrative and behavior.

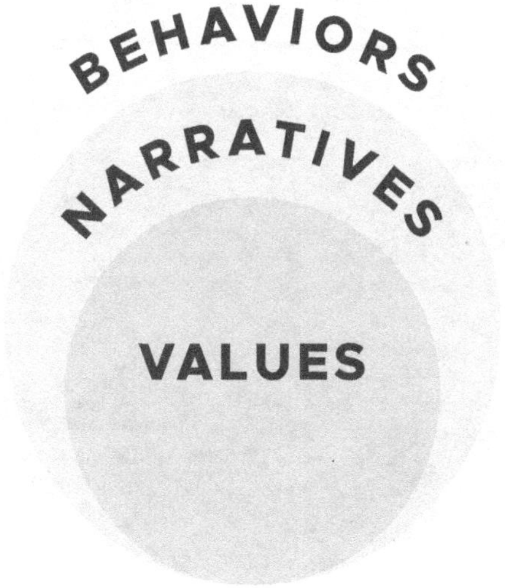

The clarity of your narrative/language and your behavior/practices is an overflow of the clarity and conviction of your values.

Culture Element 2

Language and Narratives

Narrative

- How we talk about it
- Consistency of words
- Storytelling

Pause and reflect on your church's language and narrative. Are there specific themes or patterns?

What core values do the stories reflect?

Are there core values you publicly state, but if you're honest, you don't have the stories to bring them to life?

Language and narrative (storytelling) are a powerful bridge between our core values and our practices.

Ultimately, all organizations share the common goal of continually increasing the number of people who join and participate in their unique crusade. Our language and narrative are key components in helping move people from knowing our core values (the first element of culture discussed above) to actively participating in what we do (the third element of culture discussed below).

Culture Element 3

Behaviors, Practices and Decisions

Behaviors

- What we do
- How we lay out the values

The third element of culture is where you might say, "the rubber meets the road."

You can have perfect values and a great narrative, but if your behaviors and practices are inconsistent with the story you tell, you'll struggle.

Your behaviors and practices will always be self-correcting and align to your **real** values and story.

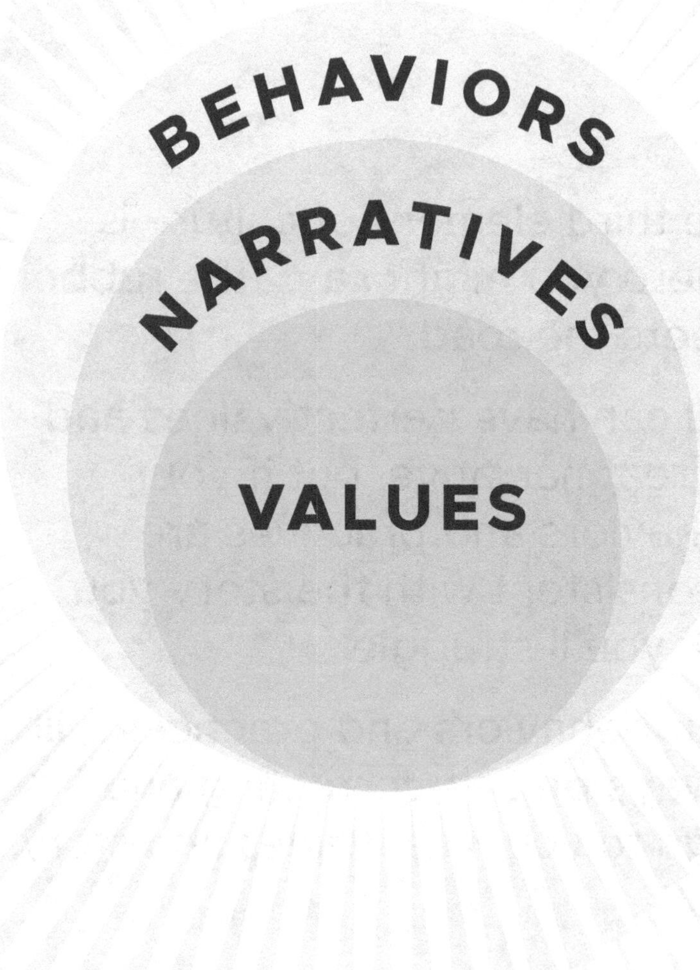
BEHAVIORS
NARRATIVES
VALUES

All three elements of culture must work synergistically to amplify and enhance one another.

Once our core values are aligned, then we have to ensure our practices and behaviors also line up.

An aligned culture is critical. And, so is your operating system...

> **Every system is perfectly designed to get the result that it does.**
>
> – W. EDWARDS DEMING

How is the culture and operating system in your church, network, and denomination creating more capacity for multiplication?

The essential tools of your operating system reveal your core priorities...

Multiplication Capacity

Operating System Essential Tool 1

Scorecard

What you measure becomes your mission.

Do you measure only inputs to your church?

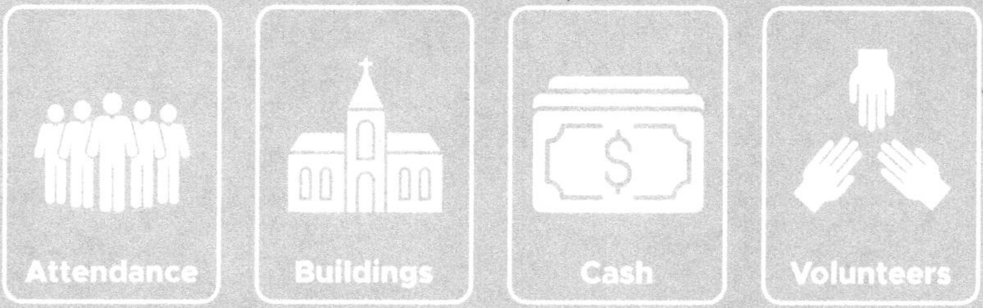

Multiplication Capacity

Operating System
Essential Tool 2

Budget

The outflow of your money reveals the heartbeat of your mission.

Multiplication Capacity

Operating System Essential Tool 3

Calendar

The **intentionality of your time, energy, and rhythms** of your church are the **greatest predictor** of addition or multiplication capacity.

It's like mom told you as a kid...

"You have time for what you want to do."

Time to put your theological thinking cap on...

Let's talk about one area of breakthrough as you increase your multiplication capacity.

Understanding your core ecclesiology fuels multiplication by clarifying the essentials that drive mobilization and movement.

?

What is your core, essential, minimum, ecclesiology?

(a.k.a. How do you define church?)

Setting the Bar Too High

If we set the bar **too high** and **overcomplicate church**, adding nonessential or man-made elements to define a church, then...

- We rob believers of the essence and biblical experience of the simple church.
- We make reproduction, and especially multiplication, much more difficult if not impossible.
- We dramatically shrink the pool of potential church planters.
- We move from an atmosphere of grace to one of legalism.
- We create high-control structures that tend toward institutionalism and away from movement.
- We decrease the number of gatherings which can become biblically true churches.

Finding the Right Balance

When we speak of **core ecclesiology**, we are primarily focusing on the **essential attributes of a gathering** which qualify it to be accurately titled "church", that is a "local church" like "the church of Corinth."

To the church of God in Corinth, to those sanctified in Christ Jesus and called to be His holy people, together with all those everywhere who call on the name of our Lord Jesus Christ—their Lord and ours.

1 CORINTHIANS 1:2

Considerations in Establishing an Essential Ecclesiology

1. Biblical Instruction - What does the Bible say about church?
2. Biblical Example - What practices are in play in the Bible narrative?
3. Church History - What teachings and practices do we see in church history and the early church writings?
4. Cultural Sensitivity - We must be sensitive to different cultural contexts without compromising core Biblical truths, teachings, and intentions.

Your Essential Ecclesiology

While God has not written a prescription we must follow, there is a description we must recognize and honor lest we invent our own definitions of church.

Our goal is not to prescribe what a definition of "church" should be or a universal essential ecclesiology. We do believe it is critically important to consider how the following elements fit in your ecclesiology.

In defining your essential ecclesiology, here are at least 7 traits that are wise to consider:

1. Jesus is worshipped as Lord.
2. Scripture is taught and obeyed as truth.
3. Believers gather regularly for fellowship.
4. Sacraments are practiced, including prayer, fasting, baptism, communion, etc.
5. Spiritual authority and God-ordained, biblically based leadership structures are present, credible, and active.
6. God's mission of disciple-making and servanthood are core priorities.
7. The Presence of the Spirit is active in the gathering.

Are you ready?

Good, now, let's focus on you.

Why? Because if we are going to experience a multiplication movement, it begins with us...it begins with you.

There's something important you need to know on these next few pages as you pursue movement...

It's in you!

It is unseen.

It is unstoppable.

It exists inside of you.

What's in you?
You were made to multiply.

Inside you is an unseen power and an unstoppable force that can create a movement for God's great good.

It's in you to be a Multiplier.

When Jesus said, "Go and make disciples of all nations" (Matthew 28:19), He was talking to everyday people—like you and me—inviting us to be part of something that can transform families, neighborhoods, and cities. You might feel ordinary, but there's extraordinary potential living within you to catalyze a movement.

What Is a Multiplier?

mul·ti·pli·er noun

A Multiplier is a healthy disciple-making leader who champions reproduction.

Why should you pursue the life of a Multiplier?

Simply put...

We Reproduce Who We Are and What We Do.

The Unseen Power of a Multiplier

A Multiplier Routinely Checks Four Health Gauges

Before you can reproduce a life that's healthy, you must first cultivate health yourself. Jesus "grew in wisdom and stature, and in favor with God and man" (Luke 2:52). We use four gauges—Relational, Physical, Mental, and Spiritual—to check our health and avoid drifting.

Multiplier RPMS Gauges

R (Relational): Am I investing well in family, friends, and community? Or am I drifting toward isolation?

P (Physical): Am I stewarding my body with exercise, rest, and healthy habits? Or is stress taking a toll on my health?

M (Mental / Emotional): Am I acknowledging and processing emotions? Or am I letting anxiety or discouragement fester?

S (Spiritual): Am I connecting with God that allows me to hear and do what he says? Or am I going through the motions?

Rate yourself 1 to 10 in each gauge. Identify where you're drifting.

- What is God saying to you about pursuing health as a Multiplier?
- What will you do about what He is saying?

Therefore everyone who hears these words of mine and puts them into practice is like a wise man who built his house on the rock.

MATTHEW 7:24

The Unstoppable Force of a Multiplier

A Multiplier Constantly Pursues Four Practices

Healthy disciples reproduce healthy disciples. Jesus's final words were an invitation to "Go . . . and make disciples" (Matthew 28:19). As a Multiplier, you don't just mature personally; you help others mature and multiply. Here are four outward practices to spark movement:

1. **Make Disciple Makers:** You invest in people, helping them hear from God and do what He says—then mobilize them to do the same.
2. **Establish Spiritual Community:** Relationships are catalytic for growth. Create and lead spaces for people to mature as disciple makers and find a place of belonging and mission.
3. **Mobilize New Leaders:** Spot potential in people and equip them to lead. Affirm their gifts, give them responsibility, and trust them to lead.
4. **Launch Church Expressions:** Whether micro, macro, meta, or other innovative approaches, keep birthing new expressions of church to reach more people for Jesus.

If you will do these simple practices of a Multiplier over and over for a lifetime it has the potential to create a multiplication movement.

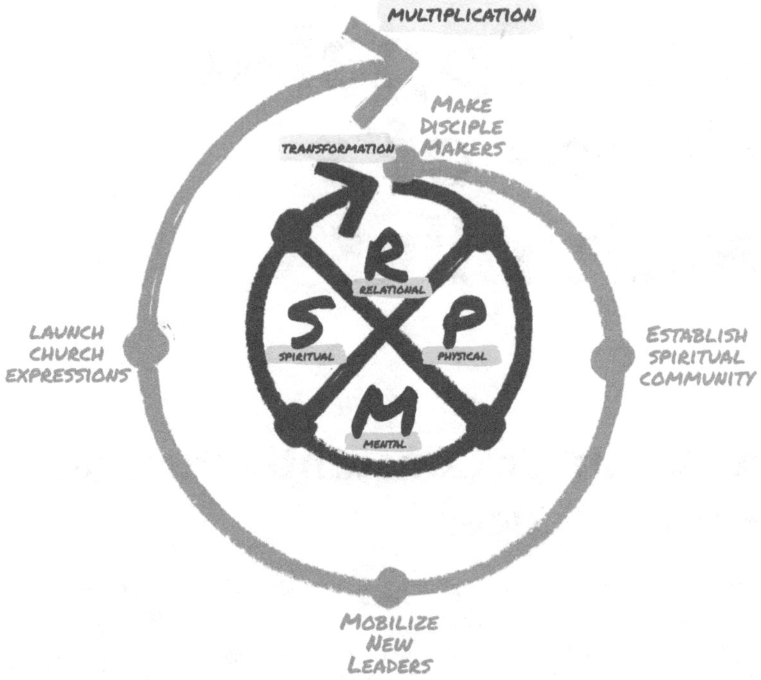

Rate yourself 1 to 10 for each practice. Identify your celebrations and challenges.

- What is God saying to you about the four practices of a Multiplier?
- What will you do about what He is saying?

But we have this treasure in jars of clay to show that this all-surpassing power is from God and not us.

2 CORINTHIANS 4:7

”

Health x Longevity = Movemental Impact

Health

Virtually anything can reproduce and multiply. In fact, cancer is just that. Something that can multiply death very quickly. But what a Multiplier is looking to do is reproduce and multiply something that is healthy. And you reproduce who you are.

Longevity

Doing the same things over and over again. This speaks to a "long obedience in the same direction", not expecting microwavable results or instant gratification. This is about building a certain kind of life more than it is about experiencing quick success.

Movemental Impact

This is about people's lives being changed far beyond what you can see or control. This is how the movement of God's Spirit did something in and through you, and there was a ripple effect, six or seven or eight generations of people beyond you.

Are you ready to begin?

What if you could **consistently check the four internal gauges** of a Multiplier and **apply the four external practices**?

Imagine the impact—not just on yourself, but on those around you. By embracing these steps, you won't just see change; you'll spark **transformation** and **ignite multiplication**.

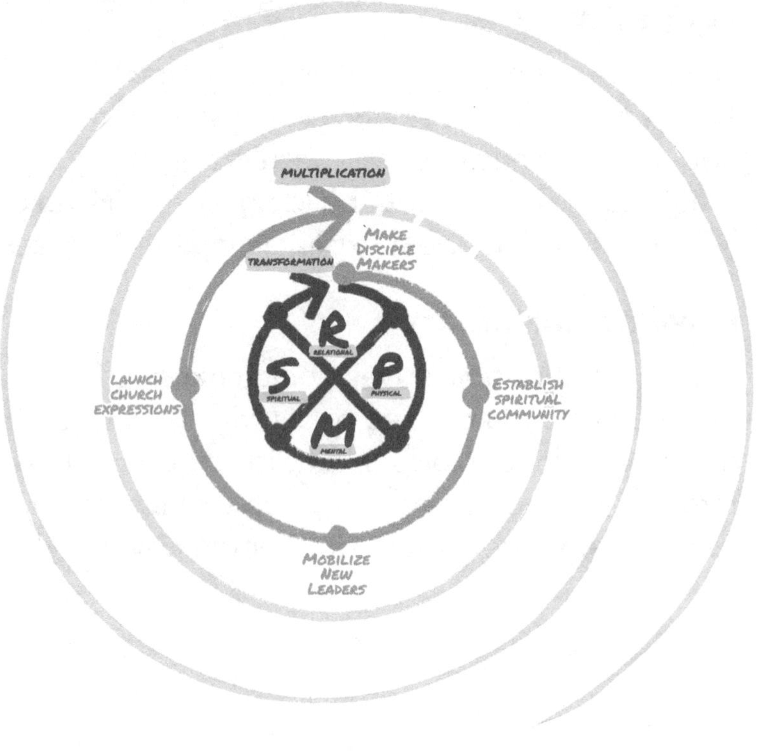

Pay attention, this is important...

But you weren't meant to do it alone!

My prayer is not for them alone. I pray also for those who will believe in me through their message, that all of them may be one, Father, just as you are in me and I am in you.

JESUS

"

The final recorded prayer of Jesus was never intended to go unanswered.

What could be the missing piece?

We know the Great Commission...

Then Jesus came to them and said, "All authority in heaven and on earth has been given to me. Therefore go and make disciples of all nations, baptizing them in the name of the Father and of the Son and of the Holy Spirit, and teaching them to obey everything I have commanded you. And surely I am with you always, to the very end of the age.

MATTHEW 28:18-20

We are called to GO!

And we know the Great Commandment...

Jesus replied: "'Love the Lord your God with all your heart and with all your soul and with all your mind.' This is the first and greatest commandment. And the second is like it: 'Love your neighbor as yourself.' All the Law and the Prophets hang on these two commandments."

MATTHEW 22:37-40

We are called to LOVE!

But We're Often Missing One Piece...

...the Great Collaboration!

May they also be in us so that the world may believe that you have sent me. I have given them the glory that you gave me, that they may be one as we are one—I in them and you in me—so that they may be brought to complete unity. Then the world will know that you sent me and have loved them even as you have loved me.

JOHN 17:21-23

We are called to Go and Love TOGETHER

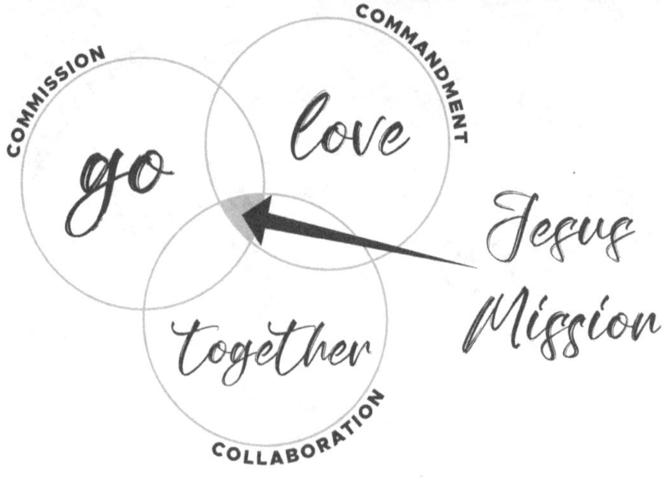

To fulfill the Jesus Mission we need to move from seeing our community through the lens of our church and become broken for the lost of our community. We must build...

Kingdom over Castle

...and it will take a shift from focusing on individual church growth (Level 3) to a collaborative approach for city transformation and gospel saturation.

But how do we take this multiplication we do on our own to the next level?
How do we sustain and scale it so that we move into exponential impact?

The answer is simple but profound: church planting networks.

1. **RESULTS Benefit:** Networks Focus on Clear Outcomes
2. **RELATIONAL Benefit:** Networks Produce Friends on Mission
3. **KINGDOM Benefit:** Networks Are All About God's Kingdom

The Challenge: Will You Multiply?

Multiplication is not a solo endeavor. If we want to start, sustain, and scale a true movement, we need networks. We need the results, relationships, and Kingdom impact that come from linking arms with others who share the vision.

GOING DEEPER
Read *Good, Great, Greater: Measuring What Matters on the Journey to Level 5 Multiplication* to learn more about capacity.
Visit exponential.org/books.

Summary

Section V

5 Essential Shifts

for a Return to Disciple-Making

We must shift our core mission:

1. **From Reaching to Making**
   We need to shift from just reaching people to making disciples.

2. **From Informing to Equipping**
   We need to shift from merely informing disciples to equipping disciple-makers.

3. **From Attending to Attaching**
   We need to shift from calling people to attend programs and events to leading people to truly attach to God and others.

4. **From Striving to Thriving**
   We need to shift from unhealthy striving to thriving as spirit-empowered disciples and emotionally healthy leaders.

5. **From Accumulating to Deploying**
   We need to shift from merely accumulating people into our buildings and programs to deploying disciple-making disciples to the ends of the Earth.

6 Critical Shifts

for Mobilizing God's People, God's Way

We must shift our culture:

1. **From more effort to more Jesus.**
2. **From seeing people as volunteers to seeing them as unique masterpieces with a mission.**
3. **From more guilt to more love.**
4. **From professional clergy doing the work of ministry to equipping and deploying everyday missionaries on mission.**
5. **From a program based "come and see" approach to a mission field "go and be" approach.**
6. **From more strategy to more prayer, fasting and surrender.**

Culture catalyzes your capacity for multiplication movement.

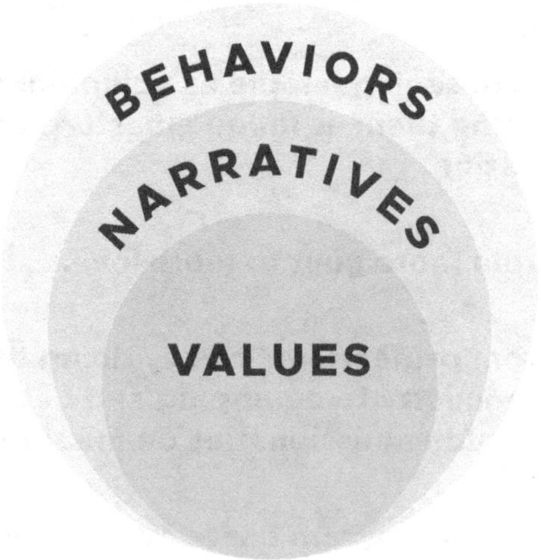

Is your culture, resources, and operating system **releasing more** disciples, missionaries, and new churches?

MOBILIZATION FLYWHEEL

Healthy mobilizing churches must strive to:

- Make disciple-making the core mission and priority of the church. Disciple-making must replace programs as the primary method of adding new disciples.
- See 100% of their members deployed as everyday missionaries to their everyday mission fields in society.
- Be "here" and "there" with a balanced approach to "come and see" and "go and be."
- Many everyday missionaries have the ability to draw people together into gatherings centered on issues of faith. Everyday missionaries should be intentional in seeking to form gatherings.

Most gatherings can reproduce and many can become new churches.

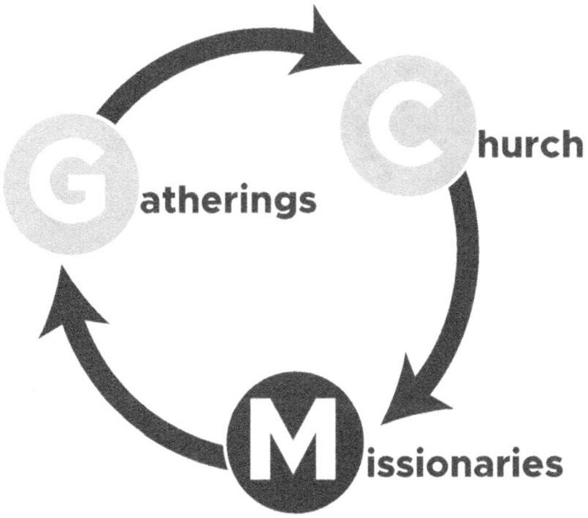

Starting New Churches

- 100% of believers have the primary or general calling to be disciples, who make disciples, wherever they are.
- 100% of believers have a secondary or unique calling that is God's special equipping to help them more effectively live out their primary calling!
- 100% of churches should prioritize helping people discover and know their primary and secondary callings.
- 100% of churches should send everyday missionaries to live out their primary and secondary callings in every crack and cranny of society.
- Most deployed everyday missionaries can form and lead gatherings within their unique circles of influence (mission fields). 100% of everyday missionaries can play a role in gatherings.
- Many gatherings can become new churches (or micro-churches) led by everyday missionaries who are bi-vocational or co-vocational.

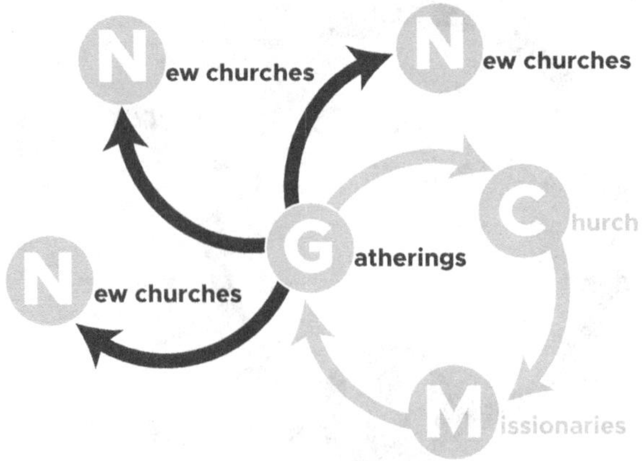

A Multiplication Movement will be accelerated through Multipliers who spark transformation and ignite multiplication. It's in you to be a Multiplier!

mul·ti·pli·er noun

A Multiplier is a healthy disciple-making leader who champions reproduction.

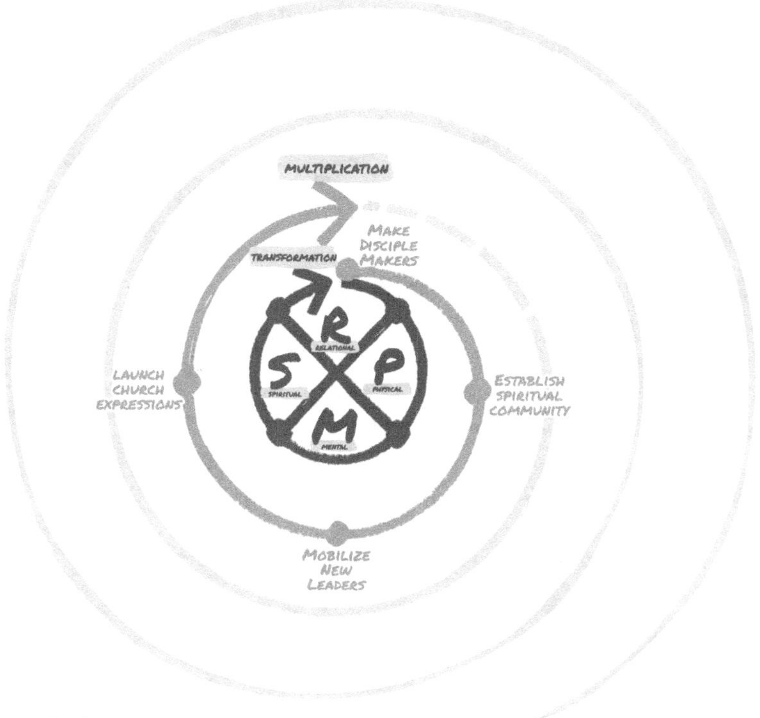

A Multiplication Movement will be accelerated through Multipliers who spark transformation and ignite multiplication. It's in you to be a Multiplier!

...the fruit of Transformation and multiplication will be in you and through you for God Kingdom and Glory!

Longevity x Health = Movemental Impact

Let's go! It's in you!

The Great Collaboration

Go–Love–Together

"...that they may be one as we are one—I in them and you in me—so that they may be brought to complete unity..."

You are a Multiplier. It's in you!

"But Jesus looked at them and said, 'With man this is impossible, but with God all things are possible.'"

MATTHEW 19:26

Now let's go make it happen—together!

Good
Great
Greater
Measuring What Matters on the Journey to Level 5 Multiplication
Noemi Chavez
Will Chung
Dave Ferguson
Jon Ferguson
Tim Hawks
Josh Husmann
Dhati Lewis
Troy & Janet McMahon
Jay Pathak
Jason Sheppard
Jason Stewart

JEFF VANDERSTELT
ONE EIGHTY
A RETURN TO DISCIPLE-MAKING
FOREWORD
DAVE FERGUSON

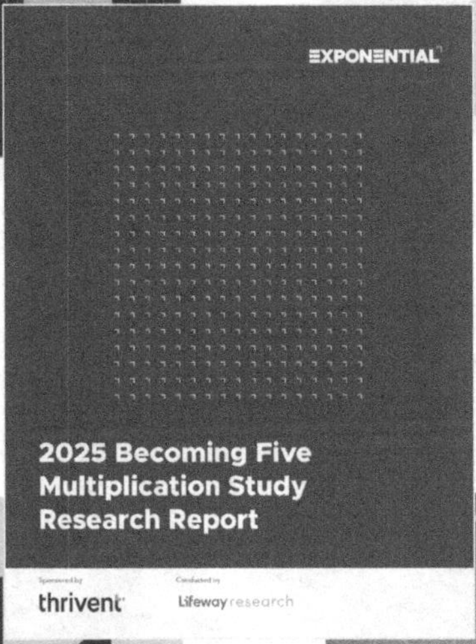
EXPONENTIAL
2025 Becoming Five Multiplication Study Research Report
thrivent
Lifeway research

RESOURCE KIT
MADE FOR MORE
SIX ESSENTIAL SHIFTS FOR CREATING A CULTURE OF MOBILIZATION
TODD WILSON & ROB WEGNER
AN EXPONENTIAL SERIES RESOURCE

EXPONENTIAL
THE MOBILIZATION FLYWHEEL
CREATING A CULTURE OF BIBLICAL MOBILIZATION
GATHERINGS
CHURCH
MISSIONARIES
LARRY WALKEMEYER and TODD WILSON
A MADE FOR MORE RESOURCE

Made in United States
Cleveland, OH
12 November 2025

25856347R00085